The IT Man of India
Azim Hashim Premji
Life & Times of Azim Hashim Premji

The IT Man of India
Azim Hashim Premji
Life & Times of Azim Hashim Premji

Edited by :
rahul singhal
a concerted effort : **xact**

PENTAGON PAPERBACKS

Great Personalities : Life Sketch Series-9

The IT Man of India
Azim Hashim Premji

Life & Times of Azim Hashim Premji

Compiled & Edited by :
rahul singhal
a concerted effort by :
xact ad 'n' art studio

Team Leader :
Rahul Singhal & Rohit
Team Members :
Assisted : **Daljit Kaur Gaba, Soma Kolay, Ratnakshi, Rinki**
Caricatures by : **K. V. Gautam**
Cover Illustration by : **Deepak Kumar**

The material in this book has been collated from various sources like News papers, Magazines, Printed material & Internet.

While every effort has been taken to avoid errors, the Compiler-Editor, Publisher and their Agents / Dealers are not responsible for the consequences of any action taken on the basis of this book.

First Published : 2002

© Reserved

ISBN 81 86830 66 9

Published by :
PENTAGON PAPERBACKS
101, AVG Bhawan,
M-3, Cannaught Place
New Delhi - 110 001
INDIA

Concept & Design by :
XACT AD 'N' ART STUDIO
Delhi

Printed at :
Elegant Printers
New Delhi

PENTAGON PAPERBACKS

The IT Man of India : Azim Hashim Premji (Life & Times of Azim Hashim Premji)

From Editor

"The IT Man of India : Azim Hashim Premji (Life and Times of Azim Hashim Premji)" is a brief story of Azim Premji, a man who has integrated the country's entrepreneurial tradition with professional management, based on sound values and uncompromising integrity.

This book unfolds the dynamism of Azim Premji's life. The book furnishes an insight into the personality of Azim Premji who is a staunch follower of down to earth approach in management. The book also talks about the various aspects in the life of Azim Premji, his education, his modesty and his likings. Above all, the book narrates Premji as a man and catches his finest moments of emotions.

Colour photographs and caricatures have been added in this book to bring forth the various aspects in Azim Premji's life in a more striking, lively and interesting manner.

CONTENTS

Introduction	11
The Man	13
Gentle Antennae of Modesty	17
His Beliefs	19
High-tech Journey	21
Beyond Business	25
What He Does	27
Saga of Success	31
De-escalating Indo-Pak Tension	35
Wins Global Award	39
Seven Steps of Success	41
Throw Open the Gates	45
Drafting Technologists on Board	51
A Model to Emulate	53
Visits Munich	57
Stake Claims in US	61
About Wipro Technology	64
Launches Solutions for Publishers	65
Best Brings in the Best	67
Free of Boarder Tensions	71
Eyes on Overseas IT Firms	73
Hitting a Six Sigma	75
India's Most Valuable Company	79
Star of Asia	81
Rise in sales from Europe	83

Successor   85

First in Europe   92

Stock of Premji's Riches   95

No Recast   97

World's Billionaire   99

Fischer meets Azim Premji   101

Alliance with West Bengal Govt.   103

No China Jump   105

Meets Craig Barret   109

Chronology   111

Cartoonist's Corner   134

Azim Hashim Premji

➤ *Introduction*

Mr. Azim Premji raised his company Wipro from a little-known family business to an information technology giant. In the last quarter of 2000, Wipro - winner of a recent £5 million contract to provide IT support to the Scottish Parliament - made a profit of about Rs. 3 billion (£44 million), a rise of 77 per cent over the previous year. With an estimated fortune of billions of pounds, Premji has become one of the richest men in the world.

He has a successful businessman's nose for an opportunity. His vision and pragmatism have helped Wipro Corporation to become the 2 most competitive and successful company in India as rated by Business Today, a leading business magazine in India Today, Wipro in terms of market capitalization is among the top 10 Corporations in India.

Managing a $500 million diversified, integrated Corporation in Services, Technology Products and Consumer Products would be a challenging affair at the best of times; Mr **Azim** Premji has had to keep his conglomerate competitive and prosperous during the era of unparalleled change. **Azim** Premji rode out the rocky period. He brought in fresh professional managers and is branching out into new areas.

The Man

Mr. **Azim** Hashim Premji the Chairman of Wipro Corporation was born in 1945 in Maharashtra. He is a qualified electrical engineer. He studied at Stanford University of United States of America. Mr. **Azim** H. Premji's father started a vegetable oil company in 1945 in Maharashtra. His father died of a heart attack in 1966. At that time **Azim** Premji was studying at Stanford University of USA. **Azim** Premji had planned to join the World Bank after completing his studies. Sudden death of Premji's father forced him to abandon his plans of joining the World Bank. At the death of his father **Azim** Premji had no other option and rushed back to India to join his father's business abandoning his plans. He joined Wipro in 1966 at the age of 21. Premji achieved fame by tilling an Old Economy company toward high tech. He is a hands-on manager, spending a third of his time on sales calls. **"It helps in getting big business drawn in,"** he says of the visits. And it shows employees how this pioneer forges ahead.

He is well known for staying in mid priced hotels. He owns an ordinary Ford sedan. He is known for his relaxed demeanor. He was named one of the richest man of the world. But, in real terms, as far as his assets are concerned, Mr Premji has nothing out of the ordinary. **He has a house in Bangalore, and that makes no news as almost any middle-class family these days owns one.**

Premji prefers not to make public comments. Once newspapers carried warnings that Kashmiri militants fighting savage war against the Indian army were planning to target Azim Premji. But he refused government protection.

He is a true leader. Under his leadership, a Rs.70 million company in hydrogenated cooking fats has grown to a $500 million diversified, integrated Corporation in Services, Technology Products and Consumer Products with leadership positions in the businesses it is in. **Azim** Premji has become a role model for young entrepreneurs across the world, Mr.Azim Premji has integrated the country's entrepreneurial tradition with professional management, based on sound values and uncompromising integrity. His deputy Vivek Paul says about Azim Premji, **"The best person I've seen who has scaled himself up. He's taken it upon himself to go from being someone who inherited a factory in Amalner, Maharashtra, to being a global ambassador for India. I completely admire him for that."**

Mr. Azim Premji's strength lies in bringing together and building charged teams of high potential-high performing people.

His contact address is :-

Wipro Technologies

Doddakannelli Sarjapur Road

Bangalore 560 035

Phone : 91 (80) 8440011

Fax: 91 (80) 8440256

e-mail: info@wipro.com

"*The end objective of our 'customer-in' concept is that we want to build the voice of the customer in our products and services. This is opposite to the concept of 'product-out', which is the way the world has been operating for some time.*"

Azim Hashim Premji
1945

The Wipro Maker

During Functions

Gentle Antennae of Modesty

Leaders have to display many qualities and many of them at the same time but to resist temptation of good living and that too, when you can afford, is a difficult self control, not very common today.

Look at the kind of marriages that have taken place in the families of political and corporate leaders in the recent past, the way they live and look at these examples of simplicity and modesty. It is because of these kind of people that we are still surviving and it is this kind of people that we need most, if we have to survive with dignity as a nation. A few examples of modesty of Azim Premji are given below:

He is the founder chairman of WIPRO whose market capitalisation is competing to be number one. Once, when his driver did not reach airport, he took an auto, reached office and made no enquiry about it.

Recently he was seen in 'Bombay House' Mumbai the head quarter of Tata's - in line to collect pass to see Mr R.M. Lala.

Mr. Premji very strongly believes that the most important contributors to Wipro's success have been the articulations and faithful adherence to core values, a shared vision for the future, identification and development of Wipro leaders through clearly defined Wipro Leaders' Qualities.

A hands-on business leader with standards of excellence in everything that the Corporation does, Mr. Premji is almost fanatical about delivering value to customers and his willingness to sacrifice business and profits to hold on to "Our Promise".

Azim Premji believes that English should be India's official language.

"Excellence is about going a little beyond; beyond what is expected from others and beyond. What we expect from ourselves. Part of the need for excellence has been imposed on us by globalisation. Improvements in the quality of products and services whet the appetites of our customers for more improvement,"

HIGH-TECH JOURNEY

Azim Premji who, for a time last year, was second only to Bill Gates as the richest man in the world (based on the valuation of his company Wipro on Nasdaq). With a market capitalization of over $12bn and with Premji holding most of the shares, Wipro has shown a CAGR of 92 per cent with sales to March 2000 of $530m and an after tax profit of $69m. In any other business in India, such a rich businessman, leading such a wealthy corporation, would have the political sharks circling. But Premji claims never to have been bothered, perhaps because they know he will not submit to their demands.

Wipro also has its own campus-style city, where

almost everything is available, from a quick swim to a bank. Once you get there from the other India, you feel you are in a different world.

But what sets Premji apart from Narayan Murthy is that while Murthy created something from nothing, **Premji, in the Indian context, had the perhaps more difficult task of converting an old-fashioned Indian company into a high-tech one.**

Such a family business rarely survives the founder but, under Premji, it was to surpass anything his father has left behind. He slowly diversified the business and in the late Seventies, helped by the then government policy that forced IBM to leave the country, he diversified into personal computers.

"IBM had left the country. Microprocess mini computers had just come in the scene. The expectations of the Indian customers were increasing. We put together a team" says Premji. "We were able to source a small company in the States. Our first computer was of 2 million rupees. It was a big, big decision in 1981-82 to buy that one".

The breakthrough came in 1984 when Wipro's infotech division diversified into software. There were difficult years (particularly 1989-90) when India had severe foreign exchange problems. But following the liberalization of 1991, as Indian exports of the software industry expanded by 50 percent every year, so did Wipro.

The vegetable oil company Premji had rushed back from Stanford to run was undergoing a transformation - so much so that it moved to Bangalore.

What makes Wipro's growth fascinating is that it has brought with it a growing association with the US rather than the UK. This may be part because of Premji's initial links with the US formed at Stanford, but it also reflects the greater strength and diversity of the Indian diaspora in the US compared to the UK.

Wipro makes 65 per cent of its sales to the US. "**We have built a strong brand in the US**" says Premji. "When we first started out, our biggest problem was convincing the outside world. First, we had to sell the country, then we had to sell our company. That has been much easier in the US."

"The Indian diaspora in the US is much stronger and that help us. The role played by Indians in the US is much more prominent than in the UK. In the US, Indian companies have built up a great reputation. A third of the engineering staff in US high-tech companies are Indian. Look at the number of Indian professor in leading business schools in America. Mostly country people from the villages migrated to the UK. In the US, it has been the elite community".

"*A time of stress is always a good time for companies to become more efficient.*"

Azim Premji established Wipro Cares i.e. a foundation focused on primary education that has been set up with a corpus of Rs.1000 million. The objective of Wipro Cares is to harness the creativity, passion and sense of social responsibility of all Wipro employees to contribute to the society that we live and work in. For instance, Wipro Cares will be educating 3500 children through Child Care India. Libraries have been set up in slums, computer skills are imparted and scholarships are made available to needy students. In the short time since its inception, Wipro Cares has brought joy to many - to the children whose lives it has touched as well as the Wipro employees who have experienced the pleasure of giving.

He established Wipro's Gujarat Earthquake Relief Fund. In response to a corporate announcement requesting contribution from Wiproites to help provide relief for the earth quake victims in Gujarat, an amount of Rs 10 million was collected. After Wipro's matching contribution, the total amount available is Rs 20 million. Premji ensured that this amount is utilized for the rehabilitation work.

Mr. Azim Premji applies technology with innovation and responsibility to achieve two broad objectives:

Effectively address the business issues our customers face today.

Generate new opportunities that will help them stay ahead in the future.

He does this in three distinct areas.

His IT Services aim at empowering the enterprise. From getting e-businesses up and going to managing technology infrastructure, we are focused on helping businesses do their business better.

His Product Design Services help companies bring defect-free products to market, in time and within budget.

His Service Provider Solutions address the specialized needs of this market to offer a complete business and technology offering. Given our technological depth and breadth, we have developed a common approach that underlies all our areas of operation. Using this, we consistently deliver solutions that maximize value for our customers. This approach rests on:

A strategy where he Architects, Integrates and Manages technology services and solutions. He calls it AIM for success.

A robust offshore development methodology that offers the advantages of parallel development and reduced demand on customer resources.

A focus on the use of reusable frameworks to provide cost and time benefits.

He combines the best people, processes and technology to achieve excellent results consistently. We offer customers the advantages of:

He understands the importance of timing, of getting there before the competition. A rich portfolio of reusable, modular frameworks helps jump-start projects. Tried and tested methodology ensures that we follow a predictable, low-risk path to achieve results. Our track record is testimony to complex projects delivered within and even before schedule. According to Standish Group estimates, only 26% of worldwide projects were done on-time/on-budget. In 1999, 80% of Wipro projects were completed within schedule.

His emphasis on quality is manifested in the SEI CMM level 5 certification the very first such certification awarded to any software services company in the world. We have now taken up a Six Sigma initiative to reduce defects and cycle times in support function processes.

His teams combine cutting edge technology skills with rich domain expertise. What's equally important we share a strong customer orientation that means we actually start by listening to the customer. We're focused on coming up with solutions that serve customer requirements today and anticipate future needs.

He offers customers the advantage of being able to Architect, Integrate and Manage technology services. This means that they can rely on one, fully accountable source instead of trying to integrate disparate multi-vendor solutions.

"*We have built the entire organization
on the basis of cash flow.*"

The one thing that impresses about Wipro the most is the sense of determination that they have. When I ask them to do a difficult task and they stand up and say they will do it, they'll move heaven and earth to make sure the job's done.

Jim Shields
Director International Carriers Division
Nortel Networks UK.

Wipro Technologies is the global technology services division of Wipro Limited. (NYSE:WIT). For the last two decades, Azim Premji has successfully served the technology needs of more than 250 customers from diverse

Premji believes he is best defined by his people talented, enthusiastic and driven. Today, he has a team of over 10,500 committed people from different managerial and engineering backgrounds.

Working in 24 offices around the world, he uses powerful technologies to provide services for business transformation and product realization as well as complete solutions for the service provider market.

His alliances with leading organizations worldwide ensure that he can offer his customers a choice of best-of-breed products and technologies. A list of his partners in different areas is given below. IT Services Business Intelligence and Data Warehousing E-Procurement Cognos, Informatica, Acta, MicroStrategy, Oracle Ariba, SAP, Oracle Business Integration m-commerce webMethods Aether Systems, Content Management Supply Chain Management BroadVision, Interwoven, Artesia Customer Relationship Management Technology Infrastructure Services Siebel, Clarify Computer Associates, Cisco, Nortel, Sun Enterprise Application Integration Travel Mercator, SeeBeyond, TIBCO Cognosys Enterprise Resource Planning Web Security SAP, Oracle RSA Product Design Services Symbian, Hyundai, TSMC, Artisan, ARM, Lineo,

With Foreign Personalities

Moods

Embedded Linux Consortium, MS Embedded Developer's Forum Service Provider Solutions Agea, Nortel, Nokia, Sun, Business Object, Clarify, Crosskeys, Forte, Mercator, Neon, SAS, Siebel, signalsoft, STC, Telsurf Networks, Vitria, Webraska, Xact Ready.

"*We were able to source a small company in the States. Our first computer was 2 million rupees. It was a big, big decision in 1981-82 to buy that one*".

De-escalating Indo-Pak Tension

The IT Man of India : Azim Hashim Premji (Life & Times of Azim Hashim Premji)

When India and Pakistan appeared headed for a nuclear war, Colin Powell, the U.S. secretary of state and a former general, played a key role in talking the two parties back from the brink. But here in India, there was another new, and fascinating, set of pressures that restrained the Indian government and made nuclear war, from its side, unthinkable. Quite simply, India's huge software and information technology industry, which has emerged over the last decade and made India the back-room and research hub of many of the world's largest corporations, essentially told the nationalist Indian government to cool it. And the government got the message and sought to de-escalate ever since. This story starts with the fact that, thanks to the Internet and satellites, India has been able to connect its millions of educated, English-speaking, low-wage, tech-savvy young people to the world's largest corporations. They live in India, but they design and run the software and systems that now support the world's biggest companies, earning India an unprecedented $60 billion in foreign reserves which doubled in just the last three years. But this has made the world more dependent on India, and India on the world, than ever before.

If you lose your luggage on British Airways, the techies who track it down are here in India. If your Dell computer has a problem, the techie who walks you through it is in Bangalore, India's Silicon Valley. Ernst & Young may be doing your company's tax returns here with Indian accountants. Indian software giants in Bangalore, Azim Premji now manages back-room operations accounting, inventory management, billing, accounts receivable, payrolls, credit card approvals for global firms like Nortel Networks, Reebok, Sony, American Express, HSBC and GE Capital.

You go to the Bangalore campuses of these Indian companies and they point out: **"That's G.E.'s back room over here. That's American Express's back office over there."** G.E.'s biggest research center outside the U.S. is in Bangalore, with 1,700 Indian engineers and scientists. The brain chip for every Nokia cellphone is designed in Bangalore. Renting a car from Avis online? It's managed here.

So it was no wonder that when the State Department issued a travel advisory warning Americans to leave India because the war prospects had risen to "serious levels," all these global firms who had moved their back rooms to Bangalore went nuts.

"That day," said Vivek Paul, vice chairman of Wipro, "I had a C.I.O. [chief information officer] from one of our big American clients send me an e-mail saying: `I am now spending a lot of time looking for alternative sources to India. I don't think you want me doing that, and I don't want to be doing it.' I immediately forwarded his letter to the Indian ambassador in Washington and told him to get it to the right person."

This was a real education for India's elderly leaders in New Delhi, but, officials conceded, they got the message: loose talk about war or nukes could be disastrous for India. This was reinforced by another new lobby: the information technology ministers who now exist in every Indian state to drum up business.

"We don't get involved in politics," said Vivek Kulkarni, the information technology secretary for Bangalore, "but we did bring to the government's attention the problems the Indian I.T. industry might face if there were a war. . . . Ten years ago [a lobby of I.T. ministers] never existed."

To be sure, none of this guarantees there will be no war. Tomorrow, Pakistani militants could easily do something so outrageous and provocative that India would have to retaliate. But it does guarantee that **India's leaders will now think 10 times about how they respond, and if war is inevitable, that India will pay 10 times the price it would have paid a decade ago.**

Wins Global Award

Azim Premji's Corporate Audit function has been awarded the commitment to Quality Improvement Award instituted by the Institute of Internal Auditors, Florida, USA.

The award recognises internal auditing departments throughout the world for their current achievements and their commitment to continued improvement in the future.

It is also an recognition of the knowledge, skills and disciplines of the internal auditing staff, their commitment to carry out their mission within the organisation.

"*There is a need to invest heavily in building a good infrastructure and strengthening the power sector in India,*"

Seven Steps to Success

The IT Man of India : Azim Hashim Premji (*Life & Times of Azim Hashim Premji*)

Mr Azim Premji, a man who is known to walk the talk. Once he delivered a lecture on the topic of: Creating a Culture of Excellence.

For someone who joined Wipro in 1966 at 21, the one factor that led us to where we are today, Mr Premji said, **"is our collective obsession with excellence"**.

"Excellence is about going a little beyond; beyond what is expected from others and beyond. What we expect from ourselves. Part of the need for excellence has been imposed on us by globalisation. Improvements in the quality of products and services whet the appetites of our customers for more improvement," he said.

"Customer delight or satisfaction has become a moving target. The benchmark for what constitutes superior quality keeps moving upward. Customers want more for less, and then, a little more for a little less. This is an absolute global truth. The other part of excellence is what we impose on ourselves. So long as the standards we set for ourselves is higher than what others expect from us, we can achieve true leadership through excellence."

Mr Premji impressed upon the audience that excellence had many rewards. Apart from the end benefits that the pursuit of excellence brings, it makes the journey itself very satisfying and personally enriching. "Excellence is not a battle with others; it is a battle you play with yourself, by constantly raising the bar and stretching yourself and your team. I have personally found that this brings out the best in me," he said.

Elaborating upon the seven steps towards excellence, Mr Premji said,

First, we need to create an obsession with excellence. We must dream of excellence not only because it delivers better results, but because we truly believe in it and find it intrinsically satisfying to all of us.

Second, we need to build collective self-confidence.

Third, we must understand the difference between perfection for its own sake and excellence where time is essence.

Four, we must realise that we cannot be the best in everything we do. We must define what we are best at and what someone else can do better. Headaches shared are headaches halved.

Five, create processes that enable excellence by building strong foundation on IT, because in this complex, dynamic world, it is imperative that we use the most modern tools to keep processes updated.

Six, there is a need to create a culture of teaming. We found at Wipro that while great individuals are important, one cannot have pockets of excellence. Quality gives ample opportunities to build a culture of teaming. Cross-functional teams that are customer facing cut through an amazing amount of bureaucracy.

Seven, invest in excellence for the future. Future always seems at a distance. But it comes upon you so suddenly that it catches you by surprise, if not shock. And what constitutes excellence in the future will be significantly different from what it is today.

"A combination of evolution and acquisitions will make Wipro a global company and we are moving in that direction. Our target markets and target companies are primarily in the IT consulting, companies which bring very strong domain knowledge or certain functions in specialised areas like retail or finance insurance"

Throw Open the Gates

RISK is a concept that seems to be actively encouraged at Wipro Ltd. Years ago, Wipro started off as a hardware product company (risky), and went on to become a services major (safe) when it discovered that the Indian market was not yet ready for a homegrown brand of hardware products.

With the turn of the century, however, Wipro decided it needed to take risks once again, that it had to create software products, no matter what everyone said about Indian companies not having the required global marketing muscle.

Two years ago, while addressing a huge gathering of techies from the company, chairman Azim Premji announced that it was necessary for the company to create intellectual property.

Since then, several technologies that employees have developed over the year are displayed annually at Tech Forum. This was the start of what is known at Wipro as the Innovation Programme.

It hasn't been as easy to actually do the innovating first of all, the key people themselves had to be clear what they defined as 'innovation' and what kind of commitment and resources were needed to keep such a project going. A core team called the Council was initially formed to articulate intentions. After touring countries and companies, they decided that if any programme had to be developed, it would have to be done in-house.

The approach was specified in terms of crossing gates. Thus, the first gate is the Idea gate, where the idea originates. This is followed by the Evaluation gate, where the proposed idea is analysed thoroughly.

Once through this gate, it has to go through the Commitment gate, which allocates resources for the project. At the Development gate, the proof of concept is put up and the idea is expected to bring in the first purchase order from a customer. Once the product is launched, it goes through the Volume gate, from where it gets absorbed into the normal business and starts generating profits.

The framework and process "will help us make Innovation a predictable event in Wipro," says L Ramanath, corporate manager, innovation and mission quality, Wipro Technologies.

"Our top management is committed and helps in improving and improvising the innovation process on a continuous basis. The process guides us from idea generation to commercialisation. The process is web-enabled and we encourage employees to contribute and participate in the innovation journey," he adds. This means that any employee can come up with his or her own ideas about products and get a project in hand, provided the idea manages to pass the specified gates.

At the end of it, the employees could end up making huge gains because they have a monetary stake in the project. The scheme of profit-sharing within Wipro is as innovative for the company as perhaps the projects themselves!

Four areas were initially identified where Wipro Technologies the global technology services division of Wipro Ltd would concentrate on for software products. Content Commerce, headed by Anurag Seth, has already come out with the first version of a product named Flow-BriX, a comprehensive workflow solution for pre-press needs.

"Flow-BriX is developed to address many of the pressing needs of the publishing industry today. Flow-BriX has evolved through successful execution of workflow projects by Wipro for large publishing houses across the globe," says Ramanath. The Home Networking team is headed by Dilip Thakore, Mobile Internetworking and Collaboration is looked after by I Vijay Kumar, and Knowledge Management is headed by Rajeev VS. According to Ramanath, all of them are working on products, and all of them have got orders from customers. "If they didn't have orders they wouldn't have gone ahead. These products all have commercial possibilities," he says.

An important criteria to qualify for an innovation project is that it should have an element of risk. Two years after the first concept was articulated, the Innovation project seems to be doing well. All four streams have become self-sustaining initiatives, needing no undue financial support from the company, though Ramanath declines to give any figures. Meanwhile, the Innovation fever spread to Wipro Infotech, the IT services, solutions

and products division of Wipro Ltd. "We thought we could copy the Technologies processes at Infotech too. But that did not work. Although we are the same group, our businesses are different, cultures are different, leaders are different. So new approaches need to be taken," says Ramanath. At Wipro Infotech, the emphasis is not on futuristic technologies but on innovative solutions and services. The first initiative is to offer an IT optimisation solution to companies. Explains Ramanath, "This is a completely outsourced solution for IT departments, which all enterprises need today. What we're proposing is that the company need not buy computers and hire people; we will buy the IT equipment, post our staff on-site. When the equipment get outdated, we shall replace them, and do software upgrades. In short, we will be practically the in-house IT department of an enterprise."

So serious is the Innovation project at Wipro Infotech that there's a target: 15 per cent of revenues should come from projects taken up by the Innovations team. In fact, every business leader at Infotech has the same target. The idea is to force everyone to look for new opportunities rather than rest on their laurels. The difference in approach at the two companies is very clear. "In Technologies, we work on hundreds of technologies, so we choose specific areas to concentrate on. At Infotech, it would be too narrow to select a specific space. Areas themselves get defined over a period of time. At Technologies, Innovation is only IP-driven. Here we've seen successes in all products we have taken up."

All live projects of Wipro Technologies have at least one customer order to validate the product. In the years to come, the home networking space will become the largest among the Innovation projects, with more products coming out and more rapidly. Who knows, Wipro may well become a household name around the world.

Drafting Technologists on Board

THE India-centric global player Wipro is contemplating a major change in the composition of its board. The Chairman of Wipro Corporation, Mr Azim H Premji, addressing a CII meeting indicated that the company was trying to bring in global technologists on to the board.

He was addressing a conference on 'Corporate Strategies for Global Excellence'.

Mr Premji, however, declined to divulge more details. Instead he said, "this major shift will be known soon." Stating that he himself was not a technologist, but a qualified electrical engineer, Mr Premji emphasised the need for selecting high quality people.

Talking about the six key strategies to success, he said

customer focus, focusing on strength (core competence), achieving global excellence through competence, global sensitivity, ability to build a culture for global teaming and the quench for emerging a global leader by breaking one's own record would ultimately lead a company to great heights.

Cautioning the industrialists about the possible threat from Chinese imports, he said, "China is a real threat for the software sector too. If we do not take on this threat seriously it can devastate the small-scale sector particularly."

Exports from China during the current year stood at $300 million, while Indian software exports touched $10 billion. "They are only four years away from us. If we continue to do a good job, we can stay ahead of them," he said. He pointed out that English was a coveted language, and the education system in China and India was math-based.

When asked if Wipro would set up a development centre in Coimbatore, Mr Premji said that as long as this city lacked direct international flight connectivity, the logistics would not work and Wipro would keep away. He suggested that the industrialists could take up the matter, as getting international flights into Coimbatore would involve no investment, only a licence/permit to the operators. "The runway is big enough to accommodate international flights," he added.

A Model to Emulate

...A MODEL TO EMULATE!

It's an 18-month effort that has culminated into reality. But the initiatives started almost 20 years ago, though it was by intuition then, says Mr. Pratik Kumar, Vice-President, Talent Engagement and Development, Wipro Technologies of the company's talking of Wipro's achievement in people's processes and quality initiatives.

Wipro Technologies has been assessed at Level 5 of People Capability Maturity Model (PCMM) under the Software Engineering Institute Carnegie Melon University certification process and it's the first company in the world to win this certification.

The Quality Assurance Institute, an assessor accredited by SEI/TeraQuest, conducted the assessment for nine days covering all strategic business units and divisions of Wipro Technologies, Bangalore. The study encompassed over 6,000 employees.

In the 1990s, Wipro started the quality initiatives. Now it is the only organisation in the world to be assessed at Level 5 under both the SEI-CMM and PCMM processes. The PCMM Model is the only such framework currently in existence. It helps organisations to successfully address critical people process issues. Based on the current best practices in human resources, knowledge management and organisation development fields, the PCMM guides organisations in continuously improving their processes for more effective management and development of their work force.

The PCMM framework decisively helps organisations improve the maturity of their people practices, establishing a programme for continuous development and integration of talent development with process improvement and finally promoting a culture of excellence and innovation.

Mr Kumar explains that PCMM is a cross-functional endeavour. Wipro employees in finance, HR, technical departments have all got involved. The idea is to match organisational competencies with individual competencies. "We have to have the vision to build individual competencies into the system. We have to realise who are our business drivers and what are our people processes are and we have to review it constantly."

So, what are the gains of the certification? "There has

been a sense of extreme pride among employees. We have built a better career framework and e-enablement processes. From the industry perspective, we have managed to build trust among customers."

How is Wipro spreading the quality message among all its employees? "We have PCMM evangelists in the company to ensure that the framework of PCMM percolates into smaller businesses. These are PCMM blackbelts like our six sigma black belts," says Mr Kumar.

Mr Vivek Paul, Vice Chairman and CEO, Wipro Technologies, explains the impact of the commendation "As people and quality processes touch everything we do, it gives our customers on time, on budget project deliveries regardless of size and complexity."

"*When we first started out, our biggest problem was convincing the outside world. First, we had to sell the country, then we had to sell our company. That has been much easier in the US.*"

Azim Premji is known as richest man of India and, in spite of global losses in the high-tech sector, still is one of the wealthiest men in the world. From the edible oil and soap-company of his father, Azim Premji has developed the Wipro Technologies mixed group since 1966 with turnover in billions, which basically produces computer hardware and software for the telecommunications and financial sectors. Now Premji has formed a contact with the gotoBavaria location marketing agency for media and IT, in the Free State of Bavaria, and is considering the establishment of a software-development center in Bavaria.

With his visit on Thursday evening, the top manager

was already confronted with high-tech at the airport: The CEO of gotoBavaria, Dr. Peter Friess, fetched the highly placed foreign visitor, as befitting his status, in a new dark blue 7-series car from BMW in Munich and impressed him with the voice-control, the navigation system and various kinds of in car electronics. The billionaire was interested in the Business Accelerator, whereby Siemens is offering a lot of promising start-ups a base to do business at the airport. Mr. Premji also seemed impressed by the architecture of Munich during the drive, when passing the Landtag State Parliament building, the state opera and the Bavarian State Chancellery. Due to the pressure of a full appointment book (his departure was planned for the early morning), he gave an interview for Bavarian Television while still in the car, before participating in a tête-à-tête with the IT sector, the 4th UMTS (3G) party of gotoBavaria.

Global companies, such as Compaq, Nortel Networks or, for example, Lucent Technologies, are included among the customers of Wipro (head office in Bangalore in the south of India). The 55 year old majority stockholder Premji (75 percent of the stocks are in his possession) sees several parallels between Bavaria and his native country Karnataka in the south of India: the city of Bangalore, with six million inhabitants, will be designated as the "Silicon City of India", while Bavaria is the "Silicon Valley of Europe". However, Premji avoids comparisons with the American market, especially as he has been turning ever more toward Europe since the recession in the US market last year. "The people are exceptionally friendly and the standard of living is very high in Bavaria" says Premji.

The Chief of the Bavarian State Chancellery and supervisory board chairman of gotoBavaria, Minister of State Erwin Huber, made mention in his welcoming speech of the overwhelming cordiality of the Indian software sector during his visit to Bangalore last October. gotoBavaria had then opened its new subsidiary, where Indian contractors now are advised locally regarding their European activities. Simultaneously, they, since they came from Munich, helped the German-Indian cultural association with the establishment of an original Bavarian Oktoberfest and, four weeks later, in turn celebrated the traditional Festival of Lights "Diwali" with 300 visitors in Munich.

With its well attended UMTS (3G) parties, every six to eight weeks gotoBavaria networks within the domestic telecommunications economy and with foreign companies which want to settle in Bavaria. "In an informal round via mobile communications 'sparks' fly between two companies sometimes more rapidly than at long-winded conferences", as gotoBavaria chief Peter Friess is pleased to note. Among the 130 visitors on Thursday evening, the manager of Deutsche Telekom technical subsidiary in Munich, Robert Wagner, the financial director of the music television M-TV, Holger Letzel, the executive board member of Holtzbrinck NetworXs AG, Helmar Hipp, the manager of economic affairs of the city of Nuremberg,

Roland Fleck, the representative from West Virginia in Bavaria, Tom Darcy, the Finnish commercial attaché, Antijussi Heilala, as well as several representatives of the Bavarian State Chancellery, were also in attendance.

The Bavarian State Government formed the so-called UMTS (3G) center of competence more than a year ago, in order that a line of developmental know-how in economics and science could be collated using the four mobile communications companies Viag Interkom, Quam, Deutsche Telekom and Vodafone, which are active in Munich. In a research group, with leading scientists, Bavaria initiates and supports the development of "killer applications", which should help the third generation of mobile communication achieve a fast breakthrough in the market launch at the end of this year.

Azim Premji's most important goal is to make Wipro Technologies as respected in the U.S. IT solutions markets as Accenture, EDS or IBM Global Services.

And the way he plans to do that is through Wipro's focus on embedded technologies, deep engineering and development work.

"What Accenture and the rest of the Big Five have done in terms of applications is that any CIO will truly trust these people to deliver solutions. They go to them for all their needs," Emani of Wipro says. "But in the engineering space, people don't think like that. They still think everything has to be done in-house."

Premji's goal is to get the message out that, by

partnering with Wipro, companies can focus on running their businesses and leave the hard-core engineering and product-development work to the experts in his company. "If we can reach that kind of positioning where people will trust us the way the Big Five are trusted, I will be happy," Emani says.

Enhancing your company's reputation to match those of the world's leading IT services firms is a hefty challenge, indeed. But fortunately for Emani, his company has some real firepower to back his aspirations. Wipro Technologies, after all, is the global technology services division of Wipro Limited, based in Bangalore, India.

The larger corporation, which got its start more than two decades ago in the hydrogenated cooking-fats industry and later expanded into consumer products and technology development, made a name for itself in recent years via its offshore development model, not to mention the behind-the-scenes R&D work it does for clients as big as Microsoft, Compaq, NEC and Nortel Networks. What's more, Wipro is one of only a handful of publicly held IT firms whose stock price has held up nicely since its IPO in 2000, with the stock trading at more than $37 a share in early April. It's currently the largest IT services firm in India, with a $9.6 billion U.S. market cap.

Wipro Technologies' business accounts for roughly 85 percent of the larger entity's revenues. Its solutions are broken down into three categories: IT services for enterprise customers, product-design services for hardware and software manufacturers, and solutions for service providers. And the company has a separate technology innovation group back in India that focuses solely on developing intellectual property.

"The competitive landscape is quite diverse," says Ayan Mukerji, vice president, North America, for embedded and Internet-access solutions. "But we position ourselves differently in that we are not a pureplay IP player. We use the IP to wrap around our services and offer an integrated solution."

Among the companies' IT services verticals are banking and finance, government, health care, insurance, manufacturing and retail. And the company is doing a lot of work lately developing Linux solutions, specifically on behalf of product manufacturers looking to reduce licensing costs. "In fact, we have been working with some Japanese players even at the printer level that want to build Linux-based printers," Emani says. Despite the hype over Linux in the enterprise space, Emani says it's still too early for wide adoption at that level. "We can help companies in terms of porting applications to Linux, making the performance better, etc.," Emani says. "But we are not seeing as much of an interest there. That will come over time."

Emani concedes that Wipro has a long way to go to get its message out in the United States. While he thinks the company is well-known in Silicon Valley, it needs to do more to increase brand awareness on the East Coast-

specifically in areas like Boston and New York. "Our listing in the NYSE about a year-and-a half ago has helped us a lot, but we need to increase our brand awareness."

About Wipro Technologies

Wipro is headquartered in Bangalore, India, and has 28 development centers across India, Europe and the United States. It also has 21 offices throughout the United States, Canada, Finland, France, the U.K and Taiwan. Wipro's global IT services revenue increased by 73 percent in 2001 to $380 million, resulting in $6 million in earnings. 61 percent of Wipro's IT services revenue in the fourth quarter of 2001 came from North America, where clients include General Motors, Boeing, Merrill Lynch, Sony and The Home Depot. The company's top 10 North American customers accounted for 45 percent of its revenue in 2001. In addition to IT services, the larger Wipro organization makes 15 percent of its revenue in consumer care, lighting and health-care technologies.

Azim Premji launched Flow-BriX, a comprehensive workflow solution for the pre- press publishing industry.

With the launch of Flow-BriX, Wipro has come out with a solution in the media and publishing domain to create efficiencies for clients through the deployment of innovative process consulting services.

To meet its specific needs, an organisation may typically purchase and customize a product or develop a solution from scratch. Through its great flexibility, Wipro's Flow-BriX provides customers with an end-to-end solution supporting rapid customization and integration with existing software tools and products for softproofing, pagination, editing and other publishing specific tools.

M. Divakaran, CTO, Wipro Technologies noted that the Flow-BriX framework will help publishers track, monitor and manage work more effectively, substantially reducing the time and cost of solution deployment. With Flow-BriX an organisation can define, model and remodel its processes with great ease. Using rule-based work allocation algorithms, managers and editors can automate work distribution and issue periodic reports on issues like productivity and work flow efficiency.

Flow-BriX facilitates communications between multiple software tools while enhancing employee collaboration, seamlessly coordinating every step of the publishing process. In addition, the framework enables the cost effective implementation of tailor-made solutions flexible enough to integrate either with publishing tools available in the market or with legacy systems.

The Flow-BriX framework is continually evolving to equip its customers with new abilities such as repurposing of content, cross media publishing and the management of digital assets and rights. Wipro Technologies is building alliances with the best of the breed products for pre-press processes such as soft proofing and content management.

Best Brings in the Best

Azim Premji brought Vivek Paul as Vice-Chairman and CEO in Wipro from General Electric in 1999. Vivek Paul is seen within Wipro as an acquisition man, ready to transform his company into a global software powerhouse. How many employees can call their boss' decision "stupid, stupid, stupid," and live to tell the story? An engineer in Wipro did and the boss who took it on the chin laughs about it today, saying: "Only in Wipro can you get away with that."

Vivek Paul can afford to look back with a smile. His 'stupid' decision to have a unified quality system has turned out to be a right move, as it's positioned Wipro as 'the execution engine of choice' for customers. It's given the company the confidence to go after $100 million-plus contracts; so far the preserve of IT services companies in the US.

Azim Premji has always hired young professionals. In a highly competitive recruiting environment, Azim Premji uses an optimal mix of sources to ensure lesser sourcing cost, reduced hiring time and higher joining rates. Employee referrals and the "e-recruitment" model contribute significantly towards achieving these objectives at Wipro Technologies.

At present, employee referral is the most significant source of recruitment at Wipro Technologies from less than 20% a year ago, employee referral hires have grown to about 40% of the overall lateral hires. The response to the employee referral program has grown significantly, now averaging about 750 referrals per week.

There are reasons why Wipro likes recruitment on the basis of employee referrals. Employees understanding of job requirements and the organizations culture is much better than other sources and results in more qualified referrals. "The best brings in the best and employees who are more qualified for the roles can integrate faster with Wipro culture," company sources said.

The top management is also actively involved in promoting the referral program within the organization and Chief Executive Officer, Vivek Paul's weekly communication to employees also invites them to participate in the referral programs. The employee referral process is automated, right from capture of candidates' resumes to online status information.

All open positions are advertised in the corporate intranet and also frequently promoted through internal name broadcast to all employees. The candidate has significantly better chances of a career with Wipro when referred by his or her friend or perhaps, former colleague; so referrals act as a powerful tool.

True to its culture of assimilating emerging technologies and trends, Wipro Technologies is one of the first in India to adopt web recruitment. Wipro's career site is designed with the needs of candidates and has emerged as the single hub for all candidate interactions.

Besides information about the company, the site has a job section, which contains an active list of job openings. Apart from the corporate recruitment site, Wipro has associations with leading job portals in India and abroad. The system allows candidates to update their resume and provides repeat opportunities for applying for a career with Wipro. About 25% of Wipro's lateral hires are through the web.

"*The Indian diaspora in the US is much stronger and that helps us. The role played by Indians in the US is much more prominent than in the UK. In the US, Indian companies have built up a great reputation. Mostly country people from the villages migrated to the UK. In the US, it has been the elite community*".

Free of Border Tensions

Mr. N.R. Narayana Murthy, Chief Mentor, Infosys Technologies, Mr. V. Leeladhar, Chairman and Managing Director, Union Bank of India, and Mr Azim Premji, Chairman, Wipro, attended a press conference in Mumbai. The recent Indo-Pak tensions have not impacted Wipro's order book adversely as there have been no cancellations of existing contracts, according to Mr Azim Premji.

"Tensions across the border have not had an adverse impact on our contracts so far. There have been no cancellations of existing contracts. The situation is improving though we need to wait and watch for the next two to three weeks," Mr Premji said on the sidelines of a press meet organised to announce Union Bank's tie-up with Wipro and Infosys for technological initiatives.

Asked about his company's acquisition plans, Mr Premji said, "We are working on acquisitions and have identified certain target companies which I cannot name at present. An amount of Rs 1,400 crore has also been earmarked specifically to fund these acquisitions."

Mr N.R. Narayana Murthy, Chief Mentor, Infosys Technologies, who was also present at the press conference, commenting on the collaboration between Wipro and Infosys for providing IT solutions to Union Bank, said, "I call this collaborative competition. Wipro has tremendous expertise in hardware. We have the country's best banking software. We have, over the past two years, been working with Wipro in suggesting solutions to banks. In a way, we are fierce competitors at one level and good collaborators at another."

Eyes on Overseas IT Firms

Azim Premji is aggressively looking at acquisitions of companies in the enterprise, finance and IT consulting arena. The company is eyeing the domestic as well the overseas market for prospective companies according to Mr Azim Premji. Mr Premji was speaking on the sidelines of the Union bank of India's press meet.

"A combination of evolution and acquisitions will make Wipro a global company and we are moving in that direction. Our target markets and target companies are primarily in the IT consulting, companies which bring very strong domain knowledge or certain functions in specialised areas like retail or finance insurance, said Mr

Premji.

He also added that other areas they were scouting for acquisitions were the enterprise sector is and acquisitions "which can give us strong brand in such specialised services." Wipro has been looking to acquire an American consulting company, mainly in the area of IT consulting, to give it a front-end in the US market. Talks have been on with various target companies for over two years now but no deal has been concluded so far. Names of Big five consulting firms and also tier two IT consulting firms ranging from Deloitte & Touche, Sapient and TMNG have been doing the rounds.

According to Mr Premji, the company would either use the full amount of Rs 1,400 crore cash surplus or a part of it for the acquisition of the companies. "The objective for maintaining this cash position is primarily for strategic acquisitions. We might use a part of the Rs 1,400 crore or the full amount for acquisition," he added.

"Whenever we conclude that cash with us cannot be used for enhancing the shareholder value, we will evaluate the quantum to be returned to the shareholders," Mr Premji said in the annual report, while stressing that the horde of cash is primarily meant for acquisitions.

Hitting a Six Sigma

Mr. Premji was the Prime drive behind Wipro's decision to achieve "Six Sigma" status in the next six years. In his address to the top management of Wipro Corporation on May 2, 1997, he said, "The end objective of our 'customer-in' concept is that we want to build the voice of the customer in our products and services. This is opposite to the concept of 'product-out', which is the way the world has been operating for some time." In this journey of achieving the near defect-free products and services, Mr. Premji is very clear that as a world class organisation, what Wipro needs to be concerned about is the process, not merely the results.

In 1997, the Rs 3,468-crore Wipro Limited started implementing the Motorola-developed Six Sigma process in its businesses ranging from toilet soaps to computer peripherals.

So far, Wipro has initiated more than 1,000 projects, trained more than 150 Black Belts (Six Sigma facilitators who are taught to look for breakthroughs in projects), and generated savings of approximately Rs. 110 crore.

This was not achieved overnight. As the chart on page 4 shows, for the first year Wipro achieved no gains. Today, however, Six Sigma has benefited Wipro across businesses. For example, in its hardware business installation failures were brought down to 1 per cent from 4.5 per cent in the past. The instances of having to rework software dropped from 12 to 5 per cent. Productivity in toilet soaps increased by 100 per cent and in the printers business by 50 per cent. Most importantly, it has taken the Sigma level of the company to 5.1 Sigma from Three Sigma over the past five years. This means that the number of defects per million opportunities (DPMO) has dropped from more than 66,807 (which is the average of a company at the Three Sigma level) to 233 DPMO.

This worked at the customer end too. For example, the company provides the NAMP 3.0 software to a large Indian telecom services provider. This software links the GSM networks to the Internet. When cellphone users

wanted to access a service like a cricket score update, the service provider's requirement was 30 "pull" per second (that is a measure of a download).

When daily updates like weather had to be relayed to cellphone users then the requirement was 30 "push" per second. Wipro claims to have managed to provide 38 pull per second and 45 push per second to the service provider.

Wipro also saves on the cost of poor quality. For an average company operating at Three Sigma, the cost of poor quality could be as high as 30 per cent of sales. For a Four Sigma company, it could be between 15 and 25 per cent and for a Five Sigma company between 5 and 10 per cent of sales. As a company gets closer to Six Sigma levels, the cost of poor quality falls below 1 per cent. In Wipro's case the cost of quality is on par with Six Sigma standards.

Says C. R. Nagaraj, corporate vice president, Mission:Quality, Wipro Limited, "When liberalisation started in the early 1990s, Wipro was suddenly confronted with two challenges. First, competition came right up to our doorstep and the beginning of the software business boom made us seek clients abroad."

As a result, says Nagaraj, "Customer focus became the key and so did the efficiencies of internal operations. The urge to differentiate ourselves and add value to the customer led us to embark on a quality journey."

Buoyed by the success in its company, from April this

year, Wipro started offering Six Sigma consulting services to other companies. The company claims to have already bagged one major client and negotiations with three more clients are in the final stages. Unlike ERP, EVA, TQM and all the other management solutions that have at one time or the other risen

in popularity, Six Sigma is harder to implement. "Six Sigma is a much more rigorous methodology. Closely linked to business metrics, it produces breakthrough results by the use of statistics," says Nagaraj.

And unlike other quality processes like TQM (total quality management) or ISO 9000 which place the business process at the forefront while initiating the drive for quality, Six Sigma approaches problems from the customer's side.

India's Most Valuable Company

Business Today, a leading fortnightly business magazine in India, has ranked Wipro as India's Most Valuable Company. In their annual study of 4,894 Indian companies, done in association with the Center of Monitoring Indian Economy (CMIE), Business Today has ranked the Top 500 Indian companies, with Wipro sitting pretty at the top of the list. "...Chairman Azim Premji is convinced about the long-term value proposition of his company - which is based on technical competency, quality processes, and the advantage of offshore development" the article said. According to the article, Wipro has targeted the IT consultancy and technology strategy space and, despite the slowdown in the global economy, can still hope for a 30-35 per cent growth.

In a year that has seen many of the technology giants come crashing down, Wipro's top ranking in Business Today's study shows that a company driven by strong fundamentals like quality, integrity, and supreme customer service will always remain the favorite of investors and customers alike.

High-tech companies are suffering in India just as they are elsewhere. But no one would guess it by Azim H. Premji's relaxed demeanor. Premji, 55, owns 84% of Bangalore-based Wipro Ltd., one of India's premier software companies. He is a star of Asia and have been named among 50 leaders at the fore front of change. Wipro engineers write and develop software for multinationals such as Nokia, NEC, Cisco Systems, and Sun Microsystems.

The high-tech stock sell-off has slammed Wipro as hard as any company in Silicon Valley. Since February, 2000,

Premji's net worth has plummeted from $40 billion - which made him one of the richest men in the world-to $6.5 billion. Yet Premji is unfazed, claiming he cares little about stock market fluctuations or personal wealth.

Azim Premji reasons that "a time of stress is always a good time for companies to become more efficient." So he is streamlining his already lean organization. Wipro's prices are now marginally lower than those of competitors such as Infosys and Sapient, which helps it retain clients in hard times. Wipro's sales totaled $660 million for the year ended in March, and the company expects revenues to grow by some 50% in the current fiscal year-far less than the usual 100% annual growth but still way ahead of competitors. The fact that Wipro has diversified helps. Half its revenues come from research and development for clients such as Alcatel and General Electric. Wipro is also the leader in India in installing servers and routers from Sun and Cisco.

Rise in sales from Europe

Wipro Ltd is seeing business from its early year dip. "This quarter is a little better than the previous, " Wipro chairman and founder Azim Premji said. "The last quarter everyone really froze in their tracks, checking how bad it was. But certainly in the enterprise space order flows have started all over again, although not as big as in the third and fourth quarter of last year." "Even business from its telecom customers, which is Wipro's other sector alongside the enterprise business, was not dropping revenues" he said. In Europe in particular, sales to telecom firms were still up by some 40 per cent year-on-year. Mr. Premji said he was confident revenues would grow faster than the Indian market for software and software services exporters which is set to growth by 40 to 45 per cent this year. Wipro in April predicted that sales could top $1 billion this year, compared with $.660 million in 2000 and Mr. Premji saw no reason to revise this figure.

Wipro has been eyeing consultancy firm in the US in an attempt to complement its business there, but despite the economic slowdown, takeover targets had not yet faced the fact that their valuations have tumbled. "It's not just that valuations have dropped because of lower sales. It's also that the growth prospects for the future have fallen, which means that the intrinsic value has fallen (which should mean even lower valuations).

Successor

With his thickset jaws, curly dark hair, sharp nose and boyish smile, Vivek Paul could be a face out of Hollywood. As it happens, he is on the other side of California, in Santa Clara.

But the 43-year-old vice-chairman of India's most valuable software firm Wipro Ltd., straddles different worlds at the same time.

As chief executive officer of Wipro's high-profile global information technology services division, Paul lives in the United States, shaking hands with big customers and catching emerging software trend to turn them into orders.

On the other hand, around 80 per cent of Wipro's 10,000 strong army of engineers sit in India where the real work is done.

In 1999, Azim Premji plucked Paul from General Electric Company to be vice-chairman, sending out a loud signal that diversified Wipro had changed track from its family-run past.

Vivek Paul is widely seen as Premji's successor. Paul charts a visionary course, possibly aided by his earlier proximity to GE's celebrated-formed chairman, John "Jack" Welch.

Premji is shy, withdrawn and old-fashioned. With 84 per cent of Wipro under his control - worth nearly $6.0 billion on paper - he lets his money, and Paul do most of the talking.

The vice-chairman is Wipro's articulate, accessible face. Paul said Premji focuses on values and cultures in the organization with some check-backs, but leaves a lot, including a good bit of vision, strategy and execution, to him.

"The best thing about working with Azim is that he and I are completely different" Paul said. "He should be a great chairman and I should a great CEO." But Azim Premji remains conservative to the core. "We have built the entire organization on the basis of cash flow." Premji said. Wipro's engineers write codes for everything from boxes that run telecoms networks to applications that work payrolls.

Last week, Wipro showed a net profit of 6.68 billion rupees ($142.7 million) for 2000/01 (April/March) on sales of 30.9 billion rupees. Paul's divisions made 57 per cent of the revenue.

Paul spent 99 days last year in India."My days are extremely packed. I'd start my day at seven in the morning and be done by 10 (in the evening)", Paul told Reuters in an interview in Wipro's sprawling campus on the outskirts of Bangalore.

He says he regrets that meetings are focused and not the informal drinks he would ideally like to have with his staff. "There is no chance to shoot the breeze. That's a negative."

With just a hint of American accent, Paul speaks of meetings on projects, technologies, marketing so that he gets a feel of processes he runs from across seven oceans. As Paul spoke, four giant screens were being readied in the nearby lawns for the first year-ahead meetings Wipro's troops will have with Paul and Premji. Paul is pleased that Wipro did not make an intended acquisition in last year's overheated markets. He is also happy that Wipro stayed away from work for Internet startups two years ago, despite attractive profit margins. With "dotcom" firm falling, there is reason for cheer.

"We were fortunate enough to have got into that craze," Paul said.

He looks back on his three years at Wipro. "You have a sense of satisfaction at the distance you've come but also a frustration at not having reached as far as you'd have liked to," says the man who's had to give up hobbies like scuba diving for lack of personal time.

Paul, who says he spends a third of his time in India, half in the US and the rest in Europe and Japan, sets great store by 'time management'. His secretary's main job is calendar management.

"I'm careful about making sure every minute of the day is utilised well. I set goals and try to live up to them. I do a conscious job of time management and auditing it post facto."

While he agrees that this kind of pace is unsustainable an American employee once told him, "You guys don't work 24/7 but 36/7" he finds it worth it because "the relish of building a new business makes up for everything."

Wipro has recently built three big businesses Systems

Integration, Package Implementation and IT outsourcing against a background where "there was a real jadedness about whether new initiatives would work."

Many of Wipro's new products and services hadn't exactly worked out. Such as Cybermanager, a product for network administration, and Wipro Finance. So what Wipro has done in the past three years is "to go after initiative after initiative, building a wall of success that gives more and more traction."

In SI, Wipro landed its biggest order yet ($70 million) from UK's Lattice group. In IT outsourcing the first breakthrough came with the $20 million Thames Water deal that "will teach us all the issues of how we take on a European workforce, and the related regulatory issues," he says. The company has just rolled out another new initiative built around Microsoft's .net platform.

What does the future hold; what kind of strategy will drive Wipro Technologies? Paul is reticent. "You don't try to architect the perfect future. Whether in personal or professional life, I don't try and call the shots too far. But what you do is this: you go down a path and every single day you look around and ask yourself how you can do better, and what twists and turns you need to take. If you need to take the turn, take it without hesitation, and never look back. It's about successively making the right decision versus some grand strategy."

For Paul, Soichiro Honda's famous response when asked about the secret of his success sums it all up: "Every quarter we struggled really hard and tried to do better and after a few years when we looked back, it looked like a strategy."

One of corporate India's most articulate speakers, Paul clams up when asked anything remotely personal, saying: "My public persona is about my company and not about me." Which means topics like sibling rivalry with sister Vibha Paul Rishi of Pepsi are taboo, though he does say: "She's way more interesting than I am."

Pushed hard, he will say, "I've been very, very lucky." How so? As a kid he wanted to work in medical electronics, as he was good at biology and physics, and "Lo and behold, I ended up working in GE Medical." The same holds true for studying in the US (he has an MBA from University of Massachusetts, Amherst) and returning to work in India. And to top it all, "I had great bosses all my life. I always learnt a lot from them."

What were those lessons? Poise, from his first boss at Pepsi in Boston. "I learnt how you can influence people by just throwing energy at them, and by being really enthusiastic about what you do from my boss in Bain & Co." And then the GE bosses: John Trani, who taught him "discipline in thinking," Goran Malm whose quote "It's my pleasure to do business with you, and it's my business to do pleasure with you," makes Paul's face light up even today. From Jeff Immelt, the current GE chairman, the poise thing again, but in a different way. "How you hide your raw talent. About never overstating oneself."

"I don't get enough white space   unscheduled time with my team. Because I split time between two continents and spend a lot of time travelling, I don't have the time to build real personal relationships at a deeper level."

Besides, of course, not being able to do the MTV commercial planned at the peak of the IT mania, which would have had Wipro's senior managers warbling on air.

A slightly run down office block in Reading, some 60km west of London, may not be the most famous example of the success of the Indian software industry, but its symbolic power outshines its aesthetics. The office, which was opened by Patricia Hewitt, the UK IT minister, belongs to Wipro, one of the leading Indian software groups. The Reading office is its first software development center in Europe.

For Azim Premji, chairman of Wipro, "it represents

significant step forward in our vision in becoming a truly global company. This is the start of our European campaign.

The opening is a mark of the Indian software sector's continuing maturity and confidence. It also reflects the increased need to set up centers overseas to become closer to clients such as Thames Water, as the development work Indian companies are now doing becomes more critical.

"*The launch of Wipro Healthcare and Life Science, is in continuation of our strategy to identify growth opportunities that enhance shareholder value.*"

Stock of Premji's Riches

The news that Wipro chief Azim Premji is the third richest man in the world appears to have left Mr. Premji himself and his colleagues cold.

The reason: The riches are notional and the market cap of Wipro has been dropping continuously.

The report in a London newspaper describing Mr. Premji the third richest man was based on other newspaper reports which in turn quoted Wipro's market cap when it was at the highest, that is at 51 billion dollars.

Mr. Premji's colleagues as also the big man himself are amused at the reports. Wipro's market cap was 51 billion dollars. Since Mr. Premji holds 75 per cent of Wipro's shares it was deemed that he held wealth worth 35 billion dollars. But, the London paper described it as 35 billion pounds which makes a huge difference.

The feeling among Wipro's top brass including possibly Mr. Premji himself is that linking wealth to the holding of shares should be tempered with a realistic assessment over what a person's riches really are.

For instance, Mr. Premji has never sold even a single share of Wipro nor will he sell any in future, says the Wipro official. So, where is the question of being the third richest man in the world, the official added.

If you take the market cap into account in assessing a person's riches, is it possible for a person to remain sane if he has lost 17 billion dollars in a month (due to the continuous fall in Mr Premji's wealth from 35 billion dollars (on February 21) to 18 billion dollars now), wonder Wipro's big bosses.

It is all virtual money and makes no sense, said a Wipro official. In real terms too, as far as his assets are concerned, Mr Premji has nothing out of the ordinary. He has a house in Bangalore, and that makes no news as almost any middle-class family these days owns one.

In fact, one worrisome factor about all the news of his being rich is that somebody should not misinterpret the riches as something real and do something stupid to get at them, says a colleague.

Wipro Corporation chairman Azim Premji has ruled out a restructuring of the company in the immediate future, saying there was no plan to spin off the consumer care and lighting businesses into separate units.

"Wipro does not have a restructuring agenda in the immediate future. We have implemented and will continue to implement organisational changes to enhance focus in each of our businesses," Premji told Business Standard.

Premji was recently rated the richest Indian by Forbes magazine. Forbes estimated his personal fortune at $2.8 billion (Rs. 12,040 crore).

Premji said his Rs. 1,804 crore diversified company would focus on further globalisation of its information technology business to deliver value to its customers.

"Last year, our focus was on opening more accounts to build a customer base. This year we are focusing on increasing the penetration into the accounts where we have built a foothold while simultaneously enhancing our customer base. To supplement our Six Sigma initiative on quality, we will take necessary steps to globalise the software business even more to deliver value to our customers."

On joint ventures, Premji said Wipro's approach was to team up with global partners in areas which added value to the customer and enhance the company's shareholder value.

In this context, Premji said Wipro was open to a partnership in the Internet services business through Wipro Net. "By this, the customer would get the value of the international partner's global experience in Internet services business and the expertise of Wipro's execution base and its access to the domestic markets." On its medical systems joint venture with GE, Premji said there was no proposal from either partner to acquire shares of the other. According to Premji, investment plans during the current year would be funded through internal accruals. On the loss-making Wipro Finance, Premji said the focus was on recovery and further investment for the existing fund-based business segment. The non-fund based operations were on a strong footing and would be continued, he added.

According to 15th annual list of world's billionaires by Forbes, Microsoft's co-founders Bill Gates and Paul Allen have come out as the richest and third richest men on the earth, with stock market wizard Warren Buffet grabbing the second position.

The billionaire club swelled to 538 members this year, up from 482 last year because Forbes decided for the first time to include all billionaires.

Previously, the magazine counted only working rich or those who ran business.

As a result, Masayoshi Son of Japan, Michael Dell of USA, Silvio Berlusconi of Italy and Rupert Murdoch of USA are some of the noted billionaires that lost their top-twenty berth in this year's list. Azim Premji & family of India have come out on 42nd position.

Fischer meets Azim Premji

German foreign minister Joschka Fischer on Thursday visited software giant Wipro Corporation and called on its chairman Azim H. Premji. During their discussion, Premji outlined the potential for rapid growth of the Indian infotech industry from $3.9 billion in 1999-2000 to $50 billion in 2008.

Wipro is currently operating with several German companies including Deutsche Bank, Infineon, Baxter, Becker GMBH among others. Premji welcomed the German initiative to benefit from India's competence in software development. He conveyed to the visiting German delegation that Indian software companies do not require immigration visas or Green Cards to do business in Germany, and suggested an experiment could be taken up to empower local offices to issue German business visas valid for 18 months instead of the existing three months.

Fisher invited Premji to visit Germany and interact with other leaders to identify areas where German companies and Indian infotech industry can mutually benefit.

Alliance with West Bengal Govt.

Azim Premji-led Wipro Infotech Limited would enter into a strategic alliance with the West Bengal Electronics Industry Development Corporation Limited (WEBEL), the state government controlled IT company , for support and maintenance of Wipro's hardware in schools. Wipro president Suresh Viswani said it in the city recently after meeting the Chief Minister of the state, Buddhadeb Bhattacharjee. He told reporters that WEBEL would also be entrusted with the job of monitoring and coordinating its projects in the state.

The projects include creating an agricultural information system and school-level IT education. Wipro will be handling the students of about 100 schools along with NIIT, another big name in Indian IT industry. However, Wipro would supply the required hardware for education and training projects, Viswani said. Samir Roy, general manager of WEBEL's corporate affairs, said that an agreement has already been signed with NIIT. "We will also enter into a relationship with Wipro for putting up hardware in schools".

Scaling the Chinese wall has become something of a mantra for Indian software services companies. Ever since Infosys announced that it was looking at China for a potential development centre, most of the other software firms also made similar noises. The one exception happens to be Azim Premji.

Wipro Technologies, the global software services arm of Wipro, is of the opinion that India is the best place to do software development work. Unlike TCS, the company hasn't been very aggressive about setting up development centres outside the country.

Wipro has been non-commital about centres outside

because, as Mr Vivek Paul, Wipro's vice chairman and CEO of Wipro Technologies says, "My personal take on this is that India is going to be forever the best place to do any of this stuff. But Wipro's take is that we have to hedge our bets. Eventually we will end up having development centres outside India but we will probably be the last one there."

He says that while having a series of development centres outside India sounds good, especially when making presentations to clients, the "reality is that every country has its own problems. If you say an Indo-Pak war will blow up the entire southern India, you may have to say something about getting kidnapped by the Abu Sayef guerrillas next time you go to Philippines." When Wipro talked to some customers about having a centre in the Philippines, "some were ecstatic, others hated it."

According to him the Indian software services story is not of price alone, but also of quality, of consistency in delivery. "Our whole story is that we do it right every single time," which is very difficult to guarantee in other places. "If you look at the ability to have an employee population that you can manage with a consistency in output there is no place like India."

To him it is `people' who make the difference. Says he, "where else will you find an employee population that is willing to work as hard as here. You tell them to re-skill and they love it unlike in other parts of the world. People have real passion for technology and the ability to absorb it and yet have a modest demeanor that allows you to provide consistent delivery. That's a difficult combination to find."

This does not mean that Wipro is putting all its eggs in the India basket and eschewing the international options. The company already has development centres in places like the UK, the US, Germany, and Canada and it will add some more in the future, but as Mr. Paul says: "We will go with the flow but will be the laggards in this."

"Last year, our focus was on opening more accounts to build a customer base. This year we are focusing on increasing the penetration into the accounts where we have built a foothold while simultaneously enhancing our customer base."

Recently Intel and Wipro reached another major milestone in their relationship when they concluded a five years agreement under which Wipro will support Intel with its expertise in the core technology areas, which are of strategic interest to Intel. Intel is working closely with Wipro in the four quadrants of Intel's strategic focus viz. ia32, Itanium, Internet exchange Architecture and Personal client architecture.

Wipro sees Intel as a strategic customer and foresees this relationship to grow many fold based on mutual strengths. Wipro has considerable expertise in the areas of ASIC, board design and software development in the field of Network processors a key focus area for Intel. In a move to focus on joint promotion of key future technologies, Intel and Wipro have established COEs at Wipro in the some of these focus areas.

The focus within Wipro for e-business is very high. Many of the Wipro customers have their e-business initiative on Intel platform. To this extent Wipro-Intel relationship is of significance from E-business perspective as well.

The strategic partnership between the two companies has other dimension to it.

Wipro is one of the largest OEM's of Intel products in India. All Wipro servers, desktops and consumer PCs have Intel Inside. Also, Wipro and Intel have strong engagements in areas of solution offerings and the Synergy Server programme of Intel. Wipro recently has entered into an agreement with Intel to sell its NGN (Next Generation Networking) products in India.

A Brief
Chronology of
events in
Azim Hashim Premji's
Life

- *In 1945 Azim Premji was born in Maharashtra*
- *In 1945 his father started a vegetable oil company in Maharashtra*
- *In 1960's he went to Stanford University, USA, for studying electrical engineering*
- *In 1966 his father died of a heart attack*
- *In 1966 he rushed back from Stanford University and joined Wipro*
- *In 1981 he bought his first computer which coasted him 2 million rupees*
- *In 1984 he diversified infotech division into software*
- *In 1997 he started implementing the Motorola-developed Six Sigma process*
- *In 1999 he plucked Vivek Paul from General Electric Company to be vice-chairman*
- *In 1999 he was rated the richest Indian by Forbes magazine*
- *In 2000 he established Gujurat Earthquake Relief Fund*
- *In 2000 he started creating software products*
- *In May, 2000 German foreign minister Joschka Fischer visited Wipro Corporation*
- *In January, 2001 he opened his first software development center of Europe in London*
- *In March, 2001 newspapers carried warnings that Kashmiri militants were planning to target him*
- *In July, 2001 he entered into a five years agreement with Intel*
- *In August, 2001 Business Today ranked Wipro as India's Most Valuable Company*
- *In September, 2001 he entered into a alliance with the West Bengal Government*
- *In May, 2002 he launched solution for publishers*
- *In June, 2002 he tied-up with Union Bank for technological initiatives*
- *In July, 2002 Wipro won a global award by Institute of Internal Auditors, Florida, USA.*

In 1945, Azim Premji was
born in Maharashtra.

In 1945, his father started a vegetable oil company in Maharashtra.

In 1960's he went to Stanford University, USA, for studying electrical engineering.

In 1966, his father died of a heart attack.

In 1966, he rushed back from Stanford
University and joined Wipro.

In 1981, he bought his first computer which coasted him 2 million rupees.

In 1984, he diversified infotech
division into software.

In 1997, he started implementing the Motorola-developed Six Sigma process.

In 1999, he plucked Vivek Paul from General
Electric Company to be vice-chairman

In 1999, he was rated the richest
Indian by Forbes magazine.

In 2000, he established Gujurat Earthquake Relief Fund.

In 2000, he started creating
software products.

In May, 2000 German foreign minister Joschka Fischer visited Wipro Corporation.

In January, 2001 he opened his first software development center of Europe in London.

In March, 2001 newspapers carried warnings that Kashmiri militants were planning to target him.

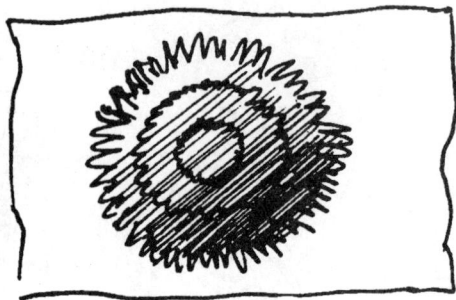

*In July, 2001 he entered into a
five years agreement with Intel.*

In August, 2001 Business Today ranked
Wipro as India's Most Valuable Company

In September, 2001 he entered into a
alliance with the West Bengal Government.

In May, 2002 he launched
solution for publishers.

In June, 2002 he tied-up with Union Bank for technological initiatives.

In July, 2002 Wipro won a global award by Institute of Internal Auditors, Florida, USA.

Cartoonist's Corner

Ajim Premji in childhood

He studied electrical engineering from Stanford University

He joined Wipro after returning from America

He diversified Infotech division of his company into Software

He established Earthquake Relief Fund during Gujarat quake

He started creating
Software Products

He has opened his Software Development Centre in London

Premji has a five-year agreement with Intel

He launched solution for publishers

His company was awarded by
Institute of Internal Auditors USA

Wipro is a giant corporation in services, technology products and consumer products.

Wipro was rated India's Most Valuable Company

Azim Premji raised Wipro from a family business to an Information Technology giant

He is considered the Richest Indian

A Bible Study

Embracing our Father's Love:

A Journey of Faith and Healing

Hope Beasley

ISBN: 979-8-89496-193-4

⟨S⟩

Staten House